9|09

P9-AFR-614

AL GORE

By Joe McGowan

People We Should Know

Gareth Stevens
Publishing

Please visit our web site at **www.garethstevens.com**.
For a free color catalog describing our list of high-quality books,
call 1-800-542-2595 (USA) or 1-800-387-3178 (Canada). Our fax: 1-877-542-2596

Library of Congress Cataloging-in-Publication Data
McGowan, Joe, 1960–
    Al Gore / by Joe McGowan.
        p. cm. — (People we should know)
    Includes bibliographical references and index.
    ISBN-10: 1-4339-1947-8   ISBN-13: 978-1-4339-1947-3 (lib. bdg.)
    ISBN-10: 1-4339-2146-4   ISBN-13: 978-1-4339-2146-9 (soft cover)
    1. Gore, Albert, 1948– —Juvenile literature. 2. Vice-Presidents—United States—
Biography—Juvenile literature. 3. Legislators—United States—Biography—Juvenile
literature. 4. United States. Congress. Senate—Biography—Juvenile literature.
5. Presidential candidates—United States—Biography—Juvenile literature. 6.
Environmentalists—United States—Biography—Juvenile literature. I. Title.
    E840.8.G65M39 2010
    973.929092—dc22 [B]   2009002349

This edition first published in 2010 by
Gareth Stevens Publishing
A Weekly Reader® Company
1 Reader's Digest Road
Pleasantville, NY 10570-7000 USA

Copyright © 2010 by Gareth Stevens, Inc.

Executive Managing Editor: Lisa M. Herrington
Senior Editor: Brian Fitzgerald
Senior Designer: Keith Plechaty

Produced by Editorial Directions, Inc.

Art Direction and Page Production: The Design Lab

Picture credits
Cover and title page: Richard Michael Pruitt/Dallas Morning News/Corbis; p. 5: Boitano
Photography/Alamy; p. 6: Jan Martin Will/Shutterstock; p. 7: Leigh Haegar/Weekly Reader; p.
8: Mario Anzuoni/Corbis; p.11: Bettmann/Corbis; p. 12: Yearbook Library; p. 13: Time & Life
Pictures/Getty Images; p. 14: AP Photo; p. 15: AP Photo; p. 17: Jeffrey Markowitz/Corbis; p. 18:
Wally McNamee/Corbis; p. 19: AP Photo/Lennox McLendon; p. 20: Time & Life Pictures/Getty
Images; p. 21: AP Photo/Carlos Osorio; p. 23: AP Photo/Ric Feld; p. 24: Larry Downing/Corbis;
p. 25: AP Photo/J. Scott Applewhite; p. 26: AP Photo/Darren Hauck; p. 27: AP Photo/Tom
Gannam; p. 28: AP Photo/Elise Amendola; p. 31: AFP/Getty Images; p. 32: AP Photo/Khue Bui;
p. 33: Reuters/Corbis; p. 34: AFP/Getty Images; p. 36: Robert King/Getty Images; p. 39: Brian
Kersey/Getty Images; p. 40: Mike Blake/Corbis; p. 41: AP Photo/Tim Larsen; p. 43: AP Photo/
Suzanne Plunkett.

All rights reserved. No part of this book may be reproduced, stored in a retrieval system, or
transmitted in any form or by any means, electronic, mechanical, photocopying, recording, or
otherwise, without the prior written permission of the copyright holder. For permission, contact
permissions@gspub.com.

Printed in the United States of America

1 2 3 4 5 6 7 8 9 14 13 12 11 10 09

TABLE OF CONTENTS

CHAPTER 1: A Great Honor 4

CHAPTER 2: Capital Childhood 10

CHAPTER 3: A Career of His Own 16

CHAPTER 4: An Invitation to Run 22

CHAPTER 5: To the White House? 30

CHAPTER 6: "Rock Star" Activist 38

Time Line. 44

Glossary. 45

Find Out More. 46

Source Notes 47

Index 48

Words in the glossary appear in **bold** type
the first time they are used in the text.

CHAPTER 1

A Great Honor

On December 10, 2007, Al Gore was especially proud. Throughout his political career, the former vice president had been honored for his accomplishments. But this award was different. On that cold night in Olso, Norway, Gore was accepting one of the world's highest honors.

He and a group of **United Nations** scientists had won the Nobel Peace Prize earlier that year. Since 1901, this award has been given to people who have worked for peace.

Al Gore's efforts helped him to win the Nobel Peace Prize.

Getting the Word Out

The audience listened carefully as Gore delivered his acceptance speech. The crowd knew that he would talk about **global warming**. Global warming is a trend that worries many world leaders. Gore and the scientists were awarded the Nobel Prize for spreading the news of the dangers they believe result from climate change. The Nobel Committee said Gore was "the single individual who has done most to create a greater worldwide understanding of the measures that need to be adopted."

Fast Fact

Past winners of the Nobel Peace Prize include former president Jimmy Carter and civil rights activist Martin Luther King Jr.

Polar bears and other animals have trouble finding food as ice melts.

A Serious Threat

In his speech, Gore said that people are "confronting a planetary emergency." He added, "The earth has a fever. And the fever is rising."

Gore believes that global warming is heating up the planet. This warming is said to create serious problems for the environment. Glaciers and other polar ice have been melting rapidly in recent years. As a result, sea levels could rise. Coastal areas may flood. Some scientists believe that higher temperatures are causing extreme weather. Examples include violent storms and long heat spells.

The Need for a Plan

Global warming is also affecting the world's wildlife. As ice melts, Arctic animals have more difficulty finding food. Some scientists worry that polar bears and other animals could be extinct in less than 10 years. Faced with the growing threat, Gore has called for a plan of action to stop global warming.

Hot Stuff

Many scientists warn that the world is getting hotter. Earth's temperature rises and falls naturally. But many scientists believe that people are causing climate changes to go to extremes. Vehicles, power plants, and factories release greenhouse gases into the air. Those gases, such as carbon dioxide, collect in a layer. They trap the sun's heat close to Earth. This process is called the **greenhouse effect**. The layer of gases acts as a window in a greenhouse does. It lets in heat but doesn't let much out. A high amount of greenhouse gases in the air causes temperatures to rise. This results in global warming.

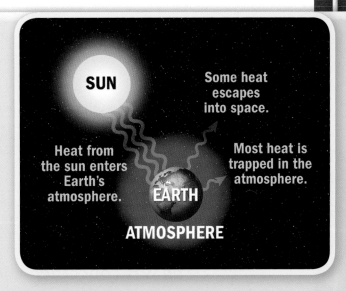

SUN

Some heat escapes into space.

Heat from the sun enters Earth's atmosphere.

Most heat is trapped in the atmosphere.

EARTH

ATMOSPHERE

Hollywood and Global Warming

Global warming has become a hot topic in Hollywood and in the movies made there. In the action thriller *The Day After Tomorrow*, New York City is overrun by a giant tidal wave and then frozen solid in a new ice age. Climate change is to blame.

Leonardo DiCaprio urges others to support the environment.

Big stars such as Leonardo DiCaprio are getting involved in the cause. In 1998, the Leonardo DiCaprio Foundation was founded. It works to increase awareness of global warming and other environmental issues.

A Green Expert

Gore has a long history of working on environmental issues. As a politician, he was concerned about the damage to **ecosystems** caused by pollution. So he supported treaties, or agreements among countries, that limit pollution. He has written best-selling books on global warming. He has also founded organizations that use the Internet to teach kids about the environment.

Only a Beginning

In 2000, Gore ran for president of the United States. He lost to Texas governor George W. Bush. Since that **campaign**, he has focused on getting the word out about what he believes to be the threat of climate change. In 2006, he starred in a movie called *An Inconvenient Truth*. The film about global warming and its theme song each won an Academy Award. This is the biggest award for movies.

Despite his awards and honors, Gore knows that his work is just beginning. Soon after his Nobel Prize win, he introduced a plan to help Americans use less energy. "I'm not finished," he told *Time* magazine.

Fast Fact

As a student at Harvard University, Gore took a course on climate science. It sparked his interest in environmental issues.

"No one should believe a solution will be found without effort, without cost, without change."

–Gore, on solving global warming at the Nobel Prize ceremony

Capital Childhood

Albert Arnold Gore Jr. was born on March 31, 1948, in Washington, D.C., the nation's capital. As the center of the United States government, Washington is a powerful city. Politicians from all over the country live and work there.

By the time Al Jr. was born, his parents, Albert and Pauline, had lived in Washington for 10 years. They had moved there in 1939. The year before, voters in Tennessee had elected Gore's father to the U.S. **House of Representatives**.

Al's father helps him shoot a bow and arrow.

A Dutiful Son

Al Gore Jr. was influenced by his parents in many ways. His father served as a congressman and in the **Senate** for more than 30 years. Unlike many Southern senators of the time, he supported equal rights for African Americans. Gore's mother was one of the first women to graduate from Vanderbilt University Law School. Al Jr. wanted to follow their bold example. He once said, "One day, I'm going to be somebody."

Fast Fact

Al Gore's father was almost nominated for the vice presidency twice.

Town and Country

Al Jr. had two childhood homes. During the school year, he lived in the capital with his parents and sister, Nancy. He spent summers working on the family farm in Carthage, Tennessee.

Back in Washington, Al Jr. attended St. Albans School. One teacher remembers him as a serious and well-rounded student. Al Jr. played football and basketball and ran track. He was also active in school government and liked to relax by painting.

Al Jr. met Mary Elizabeth Aitcheson during a school dance in 1965. She was nicknamed "Tipper." They began dating. Five years later, the two were married.

Fast Fact

Tipper Gore was nicknamed by her grandmother after a nursery rhyme, "Tippy, Tippy Tin."

Al Jr. poses for a high school yearbook photo.

A Sister and Friend

Al Gore had one sister, Nancy. She was 10 years older than he was. Nancy liked to have fun, and Al looked up to her. The Gore children had common interests. Nancy studied law and was active in the Peace Corps. The Peace Corps is a volunteer service program. It was developed by President John F. Kennedy in 1961. As an adult, Nancy smoked. She died of cancer in 1984. After her death, Gore worked to teach people about the dangers of smoking.

Al Jr. enjoys time with his sister, Nancy (right), and his parents.

On His Own

In 1966, Al Gore headed to Cambridge, Massachusetts, to attend Harvard University. At the time, the U.S. military was involved in a war in Vietnam, in southeast Asia. Like many Americans, Gore opposed the war. Protests were held on college campuses throughout the country. Gore studied government and earned his degree in 1969.

Fast Fact

Actor Tommy Lee Jones was one of Gore's roommates at Harvard. Jones later played Agent K in the *Men in Black* movies.

A Big Decision

During his last year at Harvard, Gore wondered if he should serve in the Vietnam War. He opposed the war. Yet, Gore knew that if he didn't go, he would be called anti-American. That criticism could hurt his father's career.

Out of a sense of duty to his father and to other soldiers, Gore joined the U.S. Army in 1969. He was assigned to be a military journalist after training. He was sent to Vietnam in January 1971. He wrote about the war for a newspaper called *The Castle Courier.*

Fast Fact

Gore can speak Spanish fluently.

Gore (top row, second from right) poses with soldiers during the Vietnam War.

A Troubled Time

During the 1960s, the United States was involved in the Vietnam War. Like many others, Al Gore did not think that the war was justified. Throughout the country, college students and other citizens protested the war.

People gather at a Vietnam War protest in 1966.

Vietnam is a country in Asia. During the war, it was divided into two parts. The United States supported South Vietnam. China and the Soviet Union supported North Vietnam. The war ended in 1975. By then, nearly 60,000 Americans had died. More than 150,000 Americans were injured. It is believed that more than 20 million Vietnamese people lost their lives. And another 3 million were hurt in the conflict.

In Search of Himself

Gore returned to the United States after spending less than five months in Vietnam. He was still uncertain about what career he wanted to pursue. He experimented with different careers. He also studied religion and law.

In 1976, Gore made a decision. He left law school to run for Congress. The time had come to launch his political career.

Fast Fact

Gore wrote about politics in the city of Nashville, Tennessee, for a newspaper called *The Tennessean*.

CHAPTER 3

A Career of His Own

Gore's decision to enter politics worried Tipper. She wondered how the change would affect her career and their family. At the time, the Gores had a young daughter, Karenna. Three more children would follow: Kristin, Sarah, and Albert III.

In 1976, Gore launched a campaign to become a congressman from Tennessee. Gore asked his father not to participate. He wanted voters to think of him, instead of his father. "I told him I'd vote for him," Gore's father said.

Gore talks to voters during his campaign in 1976.

A Congressional To-Do List

On the campaign trail, **candidate** Gore often asked his aides, "How'm I doin'?" In the end, he did just fine. He beat his opponent and won a seat in Congress at the age of 28. Gore was reelected three times. He served as a congressman for eight years.

In 1982, he introduced the Gore Plan. It offered ideas on how to reduce the number of nuclear weapons built in the United States. Congressman Gore also worked to provide Americans with affordable health care.

Fast Fact

Gore is a big fan of the Tennessee Titans football team.

A Moderate Member

Gore's coworkers in Congress considered him a moderate. This means he did not always agree with his political party. The United States has two main political parties: the Democrats and the Republicans. Gore is a Democrat. But he has voted with Republicans on some issues.

In Congress, Gore also focused on environmental issues. He held the first congressional hearings on climate change in 1976. He also cosponsored hearings on global warming and pollution. The environment would become a major issue in Gore's career.

Gore presents his views at a Senate hearing.

A Techno Geek

Gore has had a passion for technology throughout his career. Internet scientists Vint Cerf and Bob Kahn have written, "[Gore] was the first elected official to grasp the potential of computer communications."

As early as the 1970s, Congressman Gore supported technology as a way to grow the economy and improve education. He also studied how computers could be used to speed up the government's response to disasters.

Gore speaks with students about technology in 1996.

The Junior Senator Gore

In 1984, Gore successfully ran for the U.S. Senate. In the Senate, he continued to work on environmental and technology issues. He was described as a "genuine nerd" when it came to computers. In 1991, during his second Senate term, Gore introduced the High Performance Computing and Communications Act. The act helped to develop the "information superhighway." That was an early name for the Internet.

Fast Fact

Years before Gore supported the "information superhighway," his father sponsored a plan that created the U.S. highway system.

Al and Tipper Gore on the presidential campaign trail in 1987.

A Run for the White House

On June 29, 1987, Senator Gore announced that he would run for the U.S. presidency. He was 39 years old. He was the youngest presidential candidate since 43-year-old John F. Kennedy ran in 1960. According to the *New York Times*, political experts thought Gore was "a long shot for the Presidency."

They were right. In spite of his southern roots, Gore was unable to win support in the South. Critics accused him of running a negative campaign. After losing **party primaries** in several Southern states, he dropped out of the race.

Fast Fact

In 1991, Gore was one of only 10 Democrats to support the Gulf War against Iraq.

A Time to Rethink

It was every parent's nightmare. In 1989, Gore's six-year-old son, Albert, was struck by a car while leaving a baseball game with his parents. He was seriously injured. The Gores spent the next month in the hospital, helping their son recover.

Gore has said that the accident "changed everything." It was even a factor in his decision not to run for president again in 1992. "I would like to be president," he said at the time, "but I am also a father."

A Quiet Time

While his son recovered, Gore wrote his first book, *Earth in the Balance*. It called for a national plan to correct environmental problems. The book was a best seller. It also put Gore in the national spotlight. An invitation soon arrived that would make the spotlight even brighter.

Senator Gore carries Albert out of the hospital in 1989.

An Invitation to Run

On July 9, 1992, Bill Clinton, the governor of Arkansas, chose Senator Gore to be his running mate in the presidential election. One week later, the Democratic Party held its **national convention** in New York City. There Gore was named the party's nominee for vice president.

Clinton believed that voters would value Gore's time in Washington. Clinton thought that voters would also like Gore's experience in **foreign relations** and environmental issues.

Gore with Bill Clinton (center) and Senator Sam Nunn (left) during the 1992 campaign.

A Campaign for Youth

The Clinton–Gore team had lots of new ideas on how to run a presidential campaign. First, they worked to get young voters involved. Both candidates were in their 40s. They knew their age could help attract votes. Gore called the team "a new generation of leadership."

Fast Fact

At the age of 44, Al Gore was the youngest person ever to be elected vice president.

Bill Clinton

Born in 1946 in Hope, Arkansas, Bill Clinton served as governor of that state from 1983 to 1992. In 1992, he was elected 42nd president of the United States. He served two terms, until 2001. He is the husband of Secretary of State Hillary Clinton. Since leaving office, Bill Clinton has worked in countries throughout the world to help the poor. He created the William J. Clinton Foundation, which seeks solutions to problems such as poverty, disease, and hunger.

From the Grassroots Up

Clinton and Gore also ran a **grassroots** campaign. During one trip, the candidates and their wives traveled six days on a bus from New York City to St. Louis, Missouri. Along the way, they stopped in small towns and big cities to talk face-to-face with voters.

They worked to show voters that the Clinton–Gore team was a better choice than their opponents. President George H. W. Bush and Vice President Dan Quayle had been in office since 1989. They were running for a second term.

The Clinton–Gore Administration

On Election Day in November 1992, Bill Clinton was elected president and Al Gore was elected vice president of the United States. At the inauguration, or swearing-in ceremony, in January 1993, there was great hope. "At the edge of the 21st century, let us begin with energy and hope, with faith and discipline," Clinton said.

Before the election, there had been a war and a weak economy. The nation was ready for change. The Clinton–Gore team promised to bring it. As vice president, Gore attacked waste and abuse in government spending.

Fast Fact

President Clinton had weekly lunches with Vice President Gore, to ensure that they worked well together.

Clinton and Gore watch equipment remove outdated government manuals.

A Go-Getter

Tipper Gore is a wife and a mother, and she has worked on behalf of families, children, and the homeless. Early in her career, she worked as a newspaper photographer.

As the wife of a congressman, Tipper helped start an organization that monitors music and other media for negative material. She urged record companies to add warning labels to music that might not be suitable for young listeners. She has also supported mental health causes. In 2002, her supporters encouraged her to run for Congress. She declined.

A Fan of Research

Vice President Gore also supported research for new technologies. These included computers, robots, and communication devices. He and President Clinton even launched the first official White House web site in 1994. Gore's commitment to technology helped the economy grow. New Internet companies were formed, and millions of workers were hired.

A Second Term

In November 1996, the Clinton–Gore team was elected to a second term in office. Their main rivals had been Republican senator Bob Dole and his running mate, Jack Kemp. Youth played a role in this election. Clinton and Gore represented the younger generation and the future. Dole, who was 73, reminded many voters of the past. Clinton and Gore won by a large margin.

Fast Fact

Tipper Gore and Bill Clinton share the same birthday, August 19.

The Gores and the Clintons wave to the crowd at an event in 1996.

Vice President Gore talks to students about the environment in 1999.

Rocky Road

Over the next four years, Clinton and Gore were criticized for some of their actions. Gore faced questions about his fund-raising activities. Clinton was **impeached** in1998. That means he was charged with crimes while in public office. Gore spoke out in support of him. But many Americans wondered if Gore could be trusted.

Gore was also criticized when he met with China's leader. Critics said he shouldn't have done this because of that Asian nation's poor human rights record.

Fast Fact

One of Gore's favorite books is *The Complete Works of William Shakespeare.*

A Strong Record

Despite controversy, Gore accomplished many goals as vice president. He helped strengthen the economy. He supported advances in science and technology. He continued to work on environmental issues. He used the Internet as a tool to inform people.

Toward the end of his second term, Gore asked Congress to sign the Kyoto Protocol. This agreement required countries to lower the amount of greenhouse gases they produce. By 2000, Vice President Gore had a strong record of accomplishment. But were Americans ready for him to take the lead?

Kyoto Protocol

The Kyoto Protocol was adopted in Kyoto, Japan, on December 11, 1997. Countries that have signed this agreement are required to reduce the greenhouse gases they send into the atmosphere. The United States signed but did not adopt the treaty. However, it became a useful tool for watching the world's response to climate change.

CHAPTER 5

To the White House?

On June 16, 1999, Gore returned home to Carthage, Tennessee, to address his supporters. After his daughter Karenna introduced him to the crowd, he walked to the microphone. He thanked his friends and family for their help.

Then Gore got down to business. "With your help, I will … build an America that is not only better off, but better," he said. "And that is why today I announce that I am a candidate for president of the United States."

The Gores and the Liebermans wave to the crowd at a 2000 campaign event.

A Running Mate and an Opponent

Two months later, Gore became the Democratic Party's presidential candidate. He selected Senator Joseph Lieberman of Connecticut to be his running mate. Lieberman's candidacy also made history. He was the first Jewish person to run for vice president.

Gore's most important rival was the Republican Party candidate, George W. Bush, the governor of Texas. Bush's running mate was Dick Cheney. Cheney had a long political career in Washington.

Fast Fact

George W. Bush is the son of 41st U.S. president George H. W. Bush, whom the Clinton–Gore team defeated in 1992.

Gore greets a crowd of supporters.

On the Trail

Gore and Lieberman hit the campaign trail. They spoke about their plans for the country. Gore shared his ideas on building a strong economy and providing health care for all Americans.

The Democratic candidates also focused on finding ways to help the middle class. Those are people who earn average incomes. They're not rich and they're not poor. To the Democrats, the election was about all families sharing in the country's success and progress.

A Race to the Finish

Gore was a well-known candidate who had accomplished many things as vice president. As a presidential candidate, however, he had a hard time getting voters to like him. Many thought that he was stiff and sounded unnatural. Voters wondered if it might be time for a change from the Clinton–Gore years. On the other hand, Bush seemed relaxed and self-confident. By Election Day, the media reported the race was extremely close.

Fast Fact

Comedian Darrell Hammond has portrayed Al Gore on the TV comedy show *Saturday Night Live.*

The Debates

During the 2000 election, Al Gore and George W. Bush participated in three presidential debates. Millions of viewers watched them on TV. The candidates discussed issues facing the nation.

Bush and Gore face off in a debate in 2000.

The first televised presidential debate was in 1960. That debate was between Richard Nixon and John F. Kennedy. Since then, the debates have become an important part of presidential campaigns. In 2000, Gore called the debates "a job interview."

A Third Candidate

Ralph Nader was another candidate for president in the 2000 election. He ran for the **Green Party**. He won nearly 3 percent of the vote. Some political experts think that Nader took votes away from Gore. The election was so close that the votes Nader received may have cost Gore the presidency.

And the Winner Is …

On November 7, 2000, Americans went to the polls to cast their ballots. When the results were counted that night, voters learned they were in for a wild ride.

The race was incredibly close. The Gore–Lieberman team had captured 48 percent of the vote. So did the Bush–Cheney ticket. "I've been in politics a long time, and I don't think there's ever been a night like this one," said Gore's campaign manager, William Daley. "The race is simply too close to call."

An Uncertain Outcome

Election night came and went without a clear winner. News anchors first announced that Gore had won the presidency. Later they said Bush was the winner. Then they said there was no clear winner. Voters went to bed not knowing who had been elected. Early in the morning on November 8, Gore called Bush to admit he had lost. He soon called back to say he was not going to quit.

The election would be decided in Florida. Both candidates needed the state's 25 electoral votes in order to win. But a winner could not be named. Bush appeared to have won the state, but by a very small margin. The race there was so close that Florida law required that all the ballots had to be counted again. That was a huge job that would take election workers days to complete.

Fast Fact

After the 2000 election, Gore was a regular guest on the animated TV show *Futurama*. It may have been an attempt to show his lighter, funnier side.

❝Florida, Florida, Florida!❞

–NBC political analyst Tim Russert, explaining that the results of the vote in Florida would decide the winner of the 2000 election

Election workers recount ballots in Florida.

The Florida Recount

The goal of the recount was to determine the official winner. There were claims that some ballots had not been counted the first time. There were other claims that voting machines had not worked properly.

Ballots were sent to Tallahassee, Florida's capital, to be recounted. On November 26, Florida officially named Bush the winner of its electoral votes. But Gore argued that the count was incomplete and inaccurate. He asked the Florida Supreme Court to order a new recount. The court agreed and demanded another recount.

Tell It to the Justices

A few weeks later, the Florida recount was stopped. In the case of *Bush v. Gore*, the U.S. Supreme Court decided the recount was not legal. As a result, Gore won the popular election by about 500,000 votes. But Bush, who had already been declared the winner of Florida's electoral votes, won the presidency.

Gore disagreed with the decision. But he admitted defeat. "Tonight, for the sake of our unity of the people and the strength of our democracy, I offer my **concession**," he said.

Fast Fact

The 2000 presidential election was the subject of an HBO TV movie called *Recount*.

The Electoral College

In 2000, more people voted for Al Gore than for George W. Bush. But Bush won the election. How did that happen? Gore won the **popular vote**. But Bush received more electoral votes.

Each state has a certain number of electoral voters, based on its population. There are 538 electoral voters in all. Soon after a popular election, electoral voters cast the votes that actually decide who becomes president. A candidate needs 270 electoral votes to win the presidency. A candidate can win the popular vote but not the electoral votes needed to become president.

CHAPTER 6

"Rock Star" Activist

Since the 2000 election, Gore has not run for political office. Early in the 2004 election, many of Gore's supporters tried to convince him to run against George W. Bush again. But Gore announced that he would not enter the race.

Over the next four years, Gore's popularity grew. During the 2008 presidential primaries, polls showed Gore coming in second and third among other Democrats running for office. Yet, he hadn't even entered the race!

President Barack Obama meets with Gore to discuss energy and climate change.

A Trusted Adviser

Still, Gore has remained active in the world of politics. In 2008, he supported Barack Obama's campaign for president. Gore believed that Obama's message of change was just what the country needed.

There were even rumors that Obama would choose Gore for his vice president. Despite the talk, Gore said he did not want the job.

Fast Fact

Time magazine named Gore as a runner-up for its 2007 Person of the Year. The winner was Russian president Vladimir Putin.

Gore and director Davis Guggenheim celebrate an Academy Award for their film.

A Man with a Mission

Gore's work on climate change and other environmental issues has also kept him busy. He starred in the **documentary** *An Inconvenient Truth*. The 2006 film shows the effects of rising temperatures on the planet. The movie made Gore an unofficial spokesperson about what some believe to be the dangers of global warming. "Everywhere I go with him, they treat him like a rock star," said Davis Guggenheim, the movie's director.

Fast Fact

Melissa Etheridge won an Academy Award for her song "I Need to Wake Up," which was written for *An Inconvenient Truth* in 2006.

A Moral Issue

All this attention gave Gore celebrity status. But his goal was not fame. When *An Inconvenient Truth* won an Academy Award, Gore addressed viewers. "People all over the world, we need to solve the climate crisis. It's not a political issue," he said. "It's a moral issue."

Live Earth

In 2007, Gore helped to organize Live Earth. The concert series raised awareness of global warming. More than 150 bands in locations around the world were broadcast on TV, radio, and the Internet. Performers included Kelly Clarkson, the Police, Kanye West, and Bon Jovi. Viewers were asked to pledge their support to stop climate change.

Actor Cameron Diaz joins Gore onstage for Live Earth.

What's Next?

During the 2008 presidential campaign, Barack Obama introduced a plan to combat global warming. His plan called for using renewable energy sources. These include wind and solar (sun) energy. He acknowledged that Gore's efforts have brought more attention to the issue of climate change.

Fast Fact

Gore is a board member for Apple Inc. and serves as an adviser for Google.

Gore continues to spread the word about climate change on television. In 2008, he launched the We Campaign. The TV commercials in this campaign demand that U.S. leaders supply "truly clean energy" by 2018.

In 2007, he received an award for his work on Current TV. Current TV is a cable news network that broadcasts programs that are created by viewers.

"The future is ours: not to predict, but to create."

–Al Gore, 2008

A Family Affair

Politics and public service make up the Gore family business. Al and Tipper's oldest daughter, Karenna, worked on her father's 2000 presidential campaign. She has also worked as a journalist and has written a book on American history.

Karenna Gore Schiff (left) and Kristin Gore share their father's interest in politics and the environment.

Her sister Kristin is also a writer. She is a comedy writer for *Saturday Night Live*. She also cowrote a movie called *Arctic Tale*. The film examines how global warming may be threatening wildlife in the Arctic region.

Eyes on the Goal

Gore has proven to have influence outside of politics. Today, he prefers to work on getting the word out about global warming. A spokesperson said, "The best thing for him to do is to build support for the bold changes we have to make." Based on his career and long history of public service, Gore is just the man to inspire bold solutions.

Fast Fact

Gore's 2009 book about global warming, *Our Choice*, was printed on recycled paper.

Time Line

1948 — Albert Arnold Gore Jr. is born on March 31, in Washington, D.C.

1969 — Gore earns a degree in government from Harvard University. After graduation, he joins the U.S. Army.

1970 — Gore marries Mary Elizabeth Aitcheson, who is nicknamed Tipper.

1976 — Gore is elected to the U.S. Congress as a representative from Tennessee.

1984 — Gore is elected to the U.S. Senate. His sister, Nancy, dies of lung cancer.

1993 — Gore is sworn in as the 45th vice president of the United States.

1996 — President Bill Clinton and Vice President Gore are elected to a second term.

2000 — Gore loses the presidential election to Texas governor George W. Bush.

2007 — Gore and a group of United Nations scientists receive the Nobel Prize for their work on climate change.

Glossary

campaign: a race between candidates for an office or position

candidate: a person who is running for office

concession: an acceptance of defeat in a cause or election

documentary: a film that deals with nonfiction, or real, issues

ecosystems: communities of animals or plants interacting with their environment

foreign relations: the dealings or connections between the United States and other countries

global warming: the gradual rise in worldwide temperatures

grassroots: describing an activity that involves people and organizations at the local level

greenhouse effect: the result of gases such as carbon dioxide trapping heat in Earth's atmosphere

Green Party: a political party in the United States that supports environmental issues and citizen participation

House of Representatives: a house of the U.S. Congress, with 435 voting members elected to two-year terms

impeached: charged with wrongdoing in public office

national convention: a large gathering at which a political party officially announces its candidate for president

party primaries: state elections in which members of a political party vote for their candidate for president

popular vote: an election in which voters directly select a winner based on who wins a majority of votes

Senate: a house of the U.S. Congress, with 100 voting members elected to six-year terms

United Nations: an organization of representatives from most of the world's countries

Find Out More

Books

Gore, Al. *An Inconvenient Truth: The Crisis of Global Warming*. New York: Viking Juvenile, 2007.

McPherson, Stephanie Sammartino. *Bill Clinton*. Minneapolis: Lerner Publishing Group, 2008.

Perritano, John. *Meltdown! Global Warming Puts the World on Thin Ice*. Pleasantville, NY: Gareth Stevens, 2009.

DVDs

An Inconvenient Truth. Paramount, 2007.

Web Sites

Current TV
current.com
Find out about the latest offerings from the TV channel started by Al Gore.

The Nobel Prize
www.nobelprize.org
Read about the history of the Nobel Prize, as well as past winners.

The U.S. Government: Presidents
www.kids.gov/6_8/6_8_government_presidents.shtml
This site offers information about U.S. presidents and how government works.

Publisher's note to educators and parents: Our editors have carefully reviewed these web sites to ensure that they are suitable for children. Many web sites change frequently, however, and we cannot guarantee that a site's future contents will continue to meet our high standards of quality and educational value. Be advised that children should be closely supervised whenever they access the Internet.

Source Notes

p. 5: The Nobel Foundation, "The Nobel Peace Prize for 2007," http://nobelprize.org/nobel_prizes/peace/laureates/2007/press.html.

p. 6: Al Gore, Acceptance Speech at Nobel Peace Prize Ceremony, December 10, 2007, Olso, Norway.

p. 9 (top): Bryan Walsh, "Gore's Bold, Unrealistic Plan to Save the Planet, *Time*, July 18, 2008.

p. 9 (bottom): Gore, Acceptance Speech.

p. 11: David Maraniss and Ellen Nakashima, "Al Gore, Growing Up in Two Worlds," *Washington Post*, October 10, 1999.

p. 16: Maraniss and Nakashima, *Washington Post*.

p. 17: Maraniss and Nakashima, *The Prince of Tennessee*, 168.

p. 19: Nettime.org, "Al Gore and the Internet," http://amsterdam.nettime.org/Lists-Archives/nettime-l-0009/msg00311.html.

p. 21: Maraniss and Nakashima, *The Prince of Tennessee*, 166.

p. 23: Gwen Ifill, "The 1992 Campaign: Clinton Selects Senator Gore of Tennessee as Running Mate," *The New York Times*, July 10, 1992.

p. 25: Bartleby.com, "Bill Clinton First Inaugural Address, January 21, 1993," www.bartleby.com/124/pres64.html.

p. 29: Wikipedia, "Al Gore," www.en.wikipedia.org/wiki/Al_Gore.

p. 30: Al Gore, Presidential Candidate Announcement, June 16, 1999, Carthage, Tennessee.

p. 34: "Gore Concedes Presidential Election," CNN, December 13, 2000, http://archives.cnn.com/2000/ALLPOLITICS/stories/12/13/gore.ends.campaign/index.html.

p. 37: "Gore Concedes Presidential Election."

p. 39: "Al Gore Backs Obama for President," CNN, June 17, 2008, www.cnn.com/2008/POLITICS/06/16/gore.obama/index.html.

p. 40: William Booth, "Al Gore, Rock Star," *Washington Post*, February 25, 2007, A01.

p. 41: Al Gore, Academy Awards Ceremony, Feb. 19, 2008, Los Angeles, California.

p. 42: Gore, Academy Awards Ceremony.

Index

books 8, 21, 28
Bush, George H. W. 24, 31
Bush, George W. 9, 31, 33, 34, 35, 36, 37, 38

campaigns 16, 17, 20, 21, 22, 23, 24, 27, 28, 30, 32, 33, 39, 42, 43
Carter, Jimmy 5
Cheney, Dick 31, 34
Clinton, Bill 22, 23, 24, 25, 26, 27, 28
Clinton, Hillary 24
Current TV network 42

economy 19, 25, 26, 29, 32
elections 9, 10, 17, 23, 25, 27, 33, 34, 35, 36, 37, 38

global warming 5, 6, 8, 9, 18, 29, 40, 41, 42, 43
Gore, Albert, Sr. (father) 10, 11, 19

Gore, Albert III (son) 16, 21
Gore, Karenna (daughter) 16, 30, 43
Gore, Kristin (daughter) 16, 43
Gore, Mary Elizabeth "Tipper" (wife) 12, 16, 26, 27
Gore, Nancy (sister) 12, 13
Gore, Pauline (mother) 10, 11
Gore, Sarah (daughter) 16
greenhouse gases 7, 29
Gulf War 20

health care 17, 32

An Inconvenient Truth (film) 9, 40, 41
Internet 8, 19, 26, 29, 41

Jones, Tommy Lee 13

journalism career 14, 15

Kemp, Jack 27
Kennedy, John F. 13, 20, 33

Lieberman, Joseph 31, 32, 34
Live Earth concerts 41

Nader, Ralph 34
Nixon, Richard 33
Nobel Prize 4, 5, 9

Obama, Barack 39, 42

Putin, Vladimir 39

Quayle, Dan 24

vice presidency 11, 22, 23, 25, 26, 28, 29, 31, 39
Vietnam War 13, 14, 15

We Campaign 42

About the Author

Joe McGowan has been a reporter, writer, and editor for more than 20 years. He has worked for *Time*, *Fortune*, *Time for Kids*, *Scholastic*, and *Weekly Reader*. He also works in the theater and has produced musicals and plays on and off Broadway. He lives in New York City with his partner, Ken. He dedicates this book to his sister's dog, Lilly, who kept him company while writing.